{geography focus}

FOOD AND AGRICULTURE

{how we use the land}

Louise Spilsbury

www.raintreepublishers.co.uk
Visit our website to find out more information about **Raintree** books.

To order:
- ☎ Phone 44 (0) 1865 888112
- 🖹 Send a fax to 44 (0) 1865 314091
- 💻 Visit the Raintree Bookshop at **www.raintreepublishers.co.uk** to browse our catalogue and order online.

First published 2006 by Heinemann Library a division of Harcourt Education Australia, 20 Thackray Road, Port Melbourne Victoria 3207 Australia (a division of Reed International Books Australia Pty Ltd, ABN 70 001 002 357). Visit the Heinemann Library website at www.heinemannlibrary.com.au

Published in Great Britain in 2006 by Raintree, Halley Court, Jordan Hill, Oxford OX2 8EJ, part of Harcourt Education www.raintreepublishers.co.uk

 A Reed Elsevier company

Editorial: Moira Anderson, Carmel Heron, Diyan Leake, Patrick Catel
Cover, text design & graphs: Marta White
Photo research: Karen Forsythe, Wendy Duncan
Production: Tracey Jarrett, Duncan Gilbert
Map diagrams: Guy Holt
Technical diagrams: Nives Porcellato & Andy Craig

Typeset in 12/17.5 pt Gill Sans Regular
Origination by Modern Age
Printed and bound in Hong Kong, China by South China Printing Company Ltd

The paper used to print this book comes from sustainable resources.

National Library of Australia Cataloguing-in-Publication data:

Spilsbury, Louise.
  Food and agriculture : how we use the land.

  Includes index.
  For upper primary and lower secondary school students.
  ISBN 1 74070 279 4.

  1. Food supply. 2. Agriculture. 3. Crops. I. Title.
  (Series : Spilsbury, Louise. Geography focus).

338.191

Acknowledgements
The publisher would like to thank the following for permission to reproduce copyright material: AAP/AFP Images: p. **34**, /Paulo Santos: p. **19**; APL/Chromosohm Inc./Joseph Sohm: p. **22**, /Corbis/ Gallo Images/Anthony Bannister: p. **4**, /Martin Rogers: p. **16**, /Fulvio Roiter: p. **20**, /Jim Sugar: p. **26**; Auscape International/Wayne Lawler: p. **37**; Corbis Royalty Free: pp. **18, 28**; Getty Images/Pablo Bartholomew/ Liaison: p. **13**; Holt Studios/Nigel Cattlin: p. **32**; Imagen/Bill Thomas: p. **40**; Lonely Planet Images/Jerry Alexander: p. **12**, /Richard l'Anson: p. **8**; Photolibrary.com: p. **38**, /Age Fotostock: p. **15** (lower), /Dr P. Marazzi: p. **14**; Malie Rich-Griffith: p. **43**, /Science Photo Library /Martin Bond: p. **42**; Still Pictures/Cyril Ruoso: p. **33**, /WWI/David Woodfall: p. **30**; United States Department of Agriculture, Agricultural Research Service: p. **41** (lower). All other images PhotoDisc.

Cover photograph of wheat field reproduced with permission of PhotoDisc; inset image of kitchen for the undernourished in Bangladesh reproduced with permission of Photolibrary.com.

Every attempt has been made to trace and acknowledge copyright. Where an attempt has been unsuccessful, the publisher would be pleased to hear from the copyright owner so any omission or error can be rectified.

{contents}

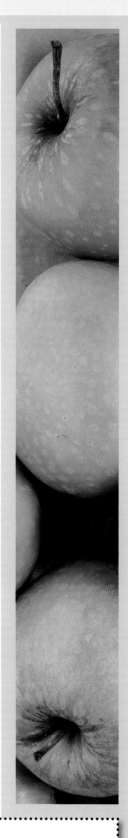

Words that are printed in bold, **like this**, are explained in the Glossary on page 46.

{feeding the world}

Human beings first appeared on Earth around 35,000 years ago. Like all other animals, early humans could only survive if they found food to eat. At first, people hunted wild animals and gathered wild plants to eat. These hunter-gatherers generally found food in one place and then moved on to other places.

The age of agriculture

Around 10,000 years ago people changed how they lived in a huge way. Family groups started to live together in small settlements, staying in one place. They started to dig areas of land to grow **crops**, such as corn, to eat. They watered and looked after the plants until they were ready to eat. They started to keep herds of useful animals such as cattle or goats in enclosed patches of land. They fed these **livestock** with wild plants or crops and protected them from danger. People drank milk from some of these animals, or killed them to eat their meat or use their skins. Over time, people started to exchange or sell any spare crops or livestock. Using or selling plants or animals you have grown or reared is called agriculture or farming.

These children's lunches are made of food grown on farms.

Growing population

Today there are still a few hunter-gatherers in places around the world. But for most people on Earth, nearly all of their food comes from agriculture. What has changed since 10,000 years ago is the number of people on the planet. Back then there were only about 4 million people on Earth. Today the **population** is over 6 billion. Some people have more food than they need but others do not have enough to eat. Feeding the world is one of the biggest challenges of the future.

Where are people hungry?

The different colours used in this map show where there are shortages of food across the world. In the countries marked red, over a third of people do not have enough food to keep them healthy. In many places in these red areas it may be that most of the people there are hungry. You can see that a lot of these countries are in Africa and Asia. In the countries marked yellow, less than one in every twenty people go hungry. These include all the countries in Europe and North America. The other two colours show places where up to 20 percent and up to 35 percent of people go hungry.

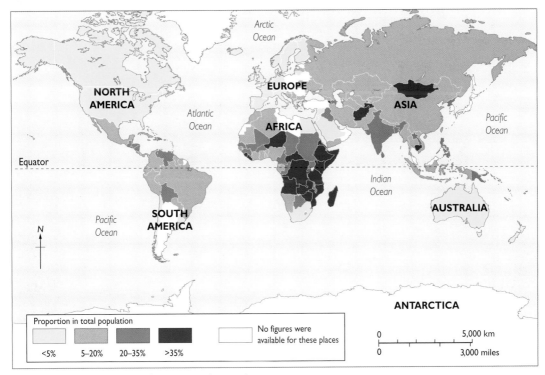

This world map shows where people are hungry.

{food chains}

Our bodies need energy to live and grow. Like all other animals we get our energy from food. You probably know that foods such as potatoes and apples come from plants. But you might not know that food made from meat, such as kebabs and bacon, would not be around without plants! That's because the **livestock** we get meat from get their energy by eating plants. We get some of this energy when we eat meat. A **food chain** is a diagram that shows how energy is passed on when an animal eats something. All food chains start with plants, but plants cannot eat. So where do plants get their energy?

Sunlight

Energy from the Sun keeps us warm and gives us light. It also makes plants grow. This is because plants use the energy in sunlight to help make their own food. They make food in their leaves using a process called **photosynthesis**. The ingredients for photosynthesis are water, sucked into the plant through its roots, and carbon dioxide, a gas from the air. Inside each leaf, sunlight jumbles up these ingredients to make sugar, which is the plant's food.

We get milk and meat from cows but the energy we get from these foods actually comes from the plants – the grass and grains – that cows eat.

The Sun's energy is trapped in the sugar. The plant releases energy from its food by combining sugar with **oxygen**, a gas in the air, inside its **cells**. Cells are the smallest building blocks of all living things. Releasing energy from food inside a living thing's cells is called **respiration**.

Chains and webs

This is a food chain. Food chains are diagrams that show where the energy from one plant goes when an animal eats it. In this example, the food chain starts with a grass plant. Plants are always the first link in a food chain because they create food inside themselves. The grass is eaten by a cow, which becomes the second link in the chain. The third link is a person who eats a burger made from the cow.

This is a food web. Food webs show how different food chains are linked. This food web shows plants that different livestock eat. The final link in this food web is people.

{croplands around the world}

Different kinds of food plants are grown around the world. All **crops** grow better in some places than in others. This is because those places naturally provide the plants with what they need.

Landscape

Landscape is the height, slope, and shape of the land. Landscape has a big effect on agriculture. For example, people grow fewer crops on mountain slopes than on flat land. This is because the soil is usually thinner, the temperature is colder, and rain runs off the land. It is also difficult for farmers to plough steep land using machines.

What is soil?

Soil is a mixture of tiny grains of rock, water, air, and humus. Humus is the name for tiny bits of dead plants and animals. The bits have been broken down by animals in soil, such as worms, and rotted by **bacteria**. Bacteria are very tiny living things. They release **nutrients** (goodness) from humus into the soil. The grains of rock release **minerals**, such as iron, which plants also need to be healthy.

Farmers in Nepal grow crops on large, flat steps called terraces that they cut into hillsides.

What do plants need?

All plants need certain amounts of water, heat, and light. These are naturally affected by the weather. Different areas of Earth have different **climates**. Climate is the usual pattern of weather a place gets, year after year.

Plants also need the right soil. Most plants take in nutrients and minerals from the soil through their roots. Soil with lots of nutrients and minerals is called **fertile** soil.

The areas on Earth with fertile soil are good for growing crops. Crops can be grown on less fertile soil if farmers use **fertilizers**. Fertilizers add nutrients to the soil.

Climates of the world

This map shows the main climate areas of the world. Arid climates are always dry. Mediterranean climates are a little wetter in winter. **Temperate** climates are cold and wet or snowy in winter, and warm and dry in summer. **Tropical** climates are always hot and sunny with heavy rainy seasons. Polar climates are very cold and dry. Mountain climates vary. It may be warm and sunny at the bottom of a mountain but very cold and cloudy at the top.

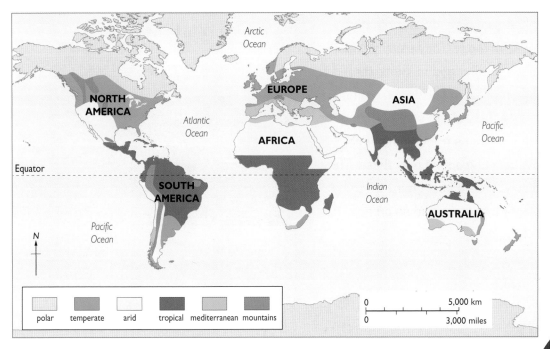

In this map you can see the world's main climate areas.

{cereals}

The most important food **crops** on our planet are **cereals**. Cereals are the grains (seeds) of different types of grasses. Types of cereals include wheat, oats, rice, millet, and maize. Farmers grow cereals such as rice to feed people. They also grow enormous amounts of grains, such as barley and maize, to feed **livestock**.

The secret of grains

The grains you might see on grass plants near where you live are usually only a few millimetres long. The grains on cereals are usually much bigger. Grains are full of **carbohydrate**, a type of sugary food that releases lots of energy soon after you eat it. They also contain **protein**, which helps us grow and heal when we are hurt. The bran (skin) around grains is made of fibre, a type of food that keeps our stomach and intestines healthy.

Changing cereals

The first wild cereals people grew in the past were different from those of today. They usually had much smaller grains. Since then farmers have made cereal grains bigger. They did this by selecting the biggest grains from the healthiest plants and planting only these. They then used the best grains from the plants that grew, and so on.

In the midwestern United States, agriculture is big business. Here, vast fields of wheat are grown and harvested with giant tractors and combine harvesters. Much of the wheat grown here is sold to feed livestock.

Grains are too tough for people to eat straight from the plant. Rice and corn grains are boiled before eating. Others, such as wheat grains, are usually ground up into flour before being cooked. Flour is used to make lots of foods such as bread, porridge, and pasta.

Growing grains

This bar chart shows how many billion tonnes of wheat, maize, and rice were grown by China and the USA in 2003. China is the top rice and wheat producer on Earth. It grows over one-quarter of all the world's rice. Its **population** is also the biggest in the world. China grows enough rice to feed its own population.

The USA is the second highest wheat producer, but **exports** nearly half of it. This means it transports and sells wheat to other countries that cannot grow enough to feed their people. The USA is the top maize producer in the world but only the eleventh highest producer of rice.

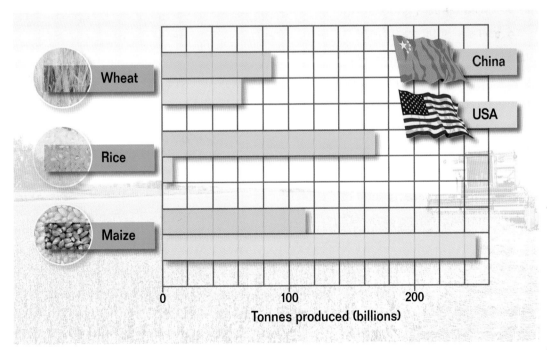

This bar chart compares wheat, rice, and maize production in China and the USA.

{case study} growing rice in Bangladesh

Bangladesh is a large country to the east of India. It is the third highest producer of rice in the world. Large parts of the country have the ideal weather and soil conditions to grow this **cereal**.

Growing conditions

Rice grows best in wet **tropical** places on **fertile** soil. Bangladesh is a wet country. Most rain falls during a five-month rainy season called the **monsoon**. The flat land in Bangladesh is only just above sea level and usually floods during the monsoon.

The rice-growing areas of Bangladesh are on the Ganges–Brahmaputra **delta**. A delta is the section of a river where it meets the sea. The delta in Bangladesh is formed where two major rivers, the Ganges and Brahmaputra, meet the Indian Ocean. River water moves so slowly here that **nutrients** and **minerals** carried along in the water drop to the bottom. Over time this fertile soil has built up in the delta.

Rice fields

Farmers in Bangladesh plant rice grains close together on small patches of land at the start of the monsoon, in May or June. When the rice plants are big enough, the farmers move them into padis (rice fields), spacing the plants a few centimetres apart.

A Bangladeshi woman is pushing seedling rice plants into the fertile mud in padis.

12

Farmers build padis with soil and mud walls around them to stop floodwater from escaping. The rice plants grow quickly and produce lots of grain if their roots remain underwater. At the end of the monsoon, about six months after planting, the farmers let water out of the padis. The grains ripen on the drying rice plants. Farmers harvest the rice by hand in November. They use machines to strip the grain from the plants and remove the outer husk. Then they put the rice in sacks and sell it.

Some farmers fit in another rice crop during the dry season by **irrigating** fields. This is when people divert water from rivers or through ditches into fields.

FACT!

Rice and other cereal plants are tall with long leaves. In the right conditions, they grow lots of grain quickly, even when planted very close together.

A rice-growing area on the Ganges–Brahmaputra delta in Bangladesh.

{fruit and vegetables}

People grow and sell a wide variety of fruit and vegetables. We eat many different parts of plants, from the leaves of spinach and the flowers of broccoli, to the fruit of tomatoes and the roots of carrots.

Around the world

Some people around the world eat mostly fresh fruit and vegetables that grow naturally nearby. For example, people in West Africa might eat yams or sweet potatoes. These are vegetables that grow in the **tropical climates**. People who live in **temperate** climates might eat different fruit and vegetables according to season. For example, they might eat asparagus in spring, raspberries in summer, plums in autumn, and cabbage in winter.

Imports and exports

Many people eat fruit and vegetables **imported** (shipped or flown in) from all around the world. Supermarkets in the UK, for example, are stocked with bananas from the West Indies, garlic from China, green beans from Africa, and mangoes from Central America. The farmers in some countries grow only fruit and vegetables that they can sell for **export**.

*Corn is used in food products such as cornflakes and as a thickener for sauces, to feed **livestock**, and in plastics, fuel, clothing, and thousands of other materials.*

Preservation

Once picked, many soft fruits and vegetables do not last long before they wilt, dry up, or start to rot. Farmers preserve these foods in different ways to keep them in good condition long after they are picked. Fruit and vegetables such as grapes, apricots, mushrooms, and tomatoes can be dried in the sun. Peas, beans, sweetcorn, and blackcurrants are often frozen and kept in freezers until they are needed.

Tomatoes under plastic

People in many parts of the world eat lots of tomatoes, fresh in salads, tinned for cooking, or processed into tomato sauce. In this picture, plastic roofs in southern Spain are helping tomatoes to grow. Tomato plants grow quickly and their fruit ripen better with extra warmth. The plastic traps the Sun's heat like the glass in a greenhouse. It means tomatoes can still be grown even in the cooler parts of the year. There is very little rain in this part of Spain so tomatoes can only grow if the land under plastic is **irrigated**.

15

{case study} going bananas!

Next time you go past the banana section in a supermarket, see if you can spot a bunch with a triangular sticker showing a palm tree and the words 'Windward Islands'. How did the bananas get from these **tropical** islands in the West Indies to your shop?

In the plantation

Large areas of tropical land covered with just one **crop** that can be harvested again and again are called **plantations**. In the Windward Islands there are thousands of small banana plantations. The **climate** and **mineral-**rich soil are good for growing banana plants. Banana plants produce fruit about six months after planting. Farmers cover growing bananas with plastic to protect them from animals and plant-like living things called **fungi** that damage the fruit.

When the bananas are three months old they are still hard and green, but they are big enough for farmers to cut them from the plant. Then the farmers wash them, put stickers on each of them and pack them carefully into boxes.

Farmers cut down 'hands' of between ten and twenty green bananas.

Export route

Boxes of bananas are sold to **exporters** whose workers sort the fruit into different sizes and check them for damage. They load the fruit onto ships. On the ships, bananas are stored in giant fridges to keep them cool. This stops them from becoming ripe on their six-day voyage. When the bananas arrive, workers unload them and take them to massive storage warehouses. Supermarkets buy their bananas from warehouses like these.

Ripe bananas

Fruit ripen when they produce a gas called ethylene. This naturally happens after they are picked and if it is warm. Workers make green bananas ripen into soft yellow fruit by pumping ethylene into banana warehouses before supermarkets take them away.

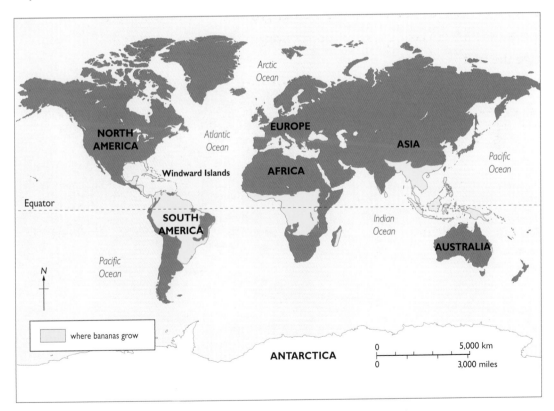

The Windward Islands are just one place where bananas are grown for export. The yellow areas of this world map show the other tropical areas where bananas grow. Where do the bananas that you eat come from?

{drink up!}

Most of the drinks people enjoy start life as parts of plants. Some plant parts are easily turned into drinks. For example, fruit such as oranges are simply squeezed or blended to make fruit juice or smoothies. Other drinks, such as tea or coffee, which also come from plants, need more complicated preparation.

Leaves

Tea is the second most popular drink in the world after water. It is made by leaving tea leaves in hot water to release their flavour. Tea leaves come from special types of camellia bushes that thrive in hills and mountains with warm, wet **climates**, such as parts of India and China.

Experienced tea **plantation** workers pick leaves from the tips of branches. In factories, the fresh leaves are processed to make the tea we buy in packets and teabags. People make green tea by first steaming, then rolling up the leaves. They make black tea by crushing fresh leaves to release their juice. The juice reacts with the air and the tea leaves turn black or dark red. Workers dry tea leaves so they will not rot when stored. Then they are packed and **exported**.

This fruit juice is being bottled in a large factory. The juice is heated up before bottling to make it stay fresh for longer.

Drinks from seeds

Coffee and cocoa are two drinks made from the seeds of trees that grow in **tropical** countries, such as Colombia and Ghana. Coffee berries are red and contain two seeds, usually called coffee beans. The beans are roasted in big ovens and ground up to release their strong flavour and smell. Cacao seeds, or cocoa beans, are left to soften in the sun and then ground up to make a dark liquid. Cocoa is the powder made from this liquid, which is used to make chocolate drinks.

FACT!

Plant parts are also used to add flavour to drinks. For example, sugar made from sugar-cane stems or sugar-beet roots is added to sweeten drinks. Cola nuts and ginger roots are used to flavour fizzy drinks.

Up to 30 seeds are removed from each yellow seed pod of the cacao tree.

{animals for food}

Farmers keep different animals to provide different foods. Some animals provide regular supplies of eggs or **dairy products**, which are foods made from milk. Others are killed for meat.

Types of animals

Around the world people keep herds of **livestock**, including sheep, cattle, goats, and buffalo. These animals need plenty of space and plants to eat. Some, such as dairy cattle, produce their best milk when they **graze** on lush, green grass. Others, such as goats and camels, can feed on tough, dry grasses and twigs. They survive even in places at the edges of mountains or deserts that are too steep or dry for other livestock.

People also keep pigs, hens, and ducks. These animals need less space and eat a wider range of foods, including leftovers. Because lots of these animals can be kept in smaller spaces, they are increasingly popular livestock across the world. There are now about 16 billion hens on Earth.

*There are over 200 different breeds of cattle around the world. Some give rich milk, while others are used for beef. Cattle also carry heavy loads for farmers and their waste is often used to **fertilize** fields.*

Livestock and religion

One thing that affects the kinds of animals people eat and keep for food is their culture. For example, followers of the religion of Islam are not allowed to eat pork, so there are few pigs in Islamic countries. Members of the Hindu religion are not allowed to harm cattle but India, where most people are Hindus, has one-fifth of all cattle on Earth. Hindus keep cattle for dairy products, but employ people of other religions to kill cattle in order to supply meat and leather to other countries.

Where are the livestock?

This world map shows the density of livestock in the world. Density is the average amount on each bit of land. In this case the amount is the average number of livestock on each square kilometre. The lightest yellow, lowest density livestock areas include large parts of North America. Many of the areas with the highest livestock density, shown in dark brown, are in a band between Europe and Asia.

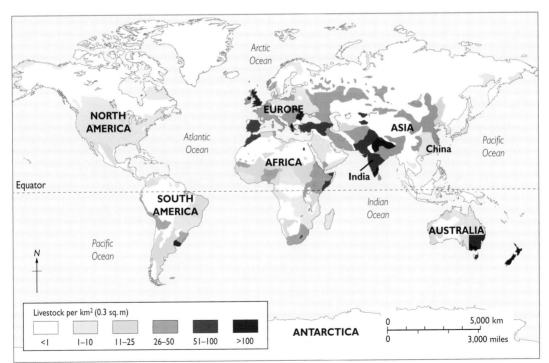

This world map shows where most livestock are kept. The largest concentrations of livestock are in India, China, and parts of Europe where most people live.

{fish farming}

Not all farming involves **crops** and **livestock**. Lots of people around the world farm fish. They raise and feed fish, such as carp, catfish, and trout, in ponds and lakes. They raise shellfish, such as prawns and oysters, in cages in the sea and even in waterlogged fields where rice grows.

Fish grow quickly in farms and lots of fish can be packed into a small area. This means farmers have a constant supply of fish to sell. Fish is an important source of **protein** for the planet's growing **population**.

Ocean and farmed fish

It takes more effort to catch wild fish than farmed fish. The numbers of wild fish in rivers, lakes, and oceans are dropping because people are **overfishing**. Overfishing is when too many fish are taken from an area of water.

*In China, fish farming is often connected with livestock farming. For example, farmers put pig manure in ponds. This encourages the growth of plant-like living things called **algae**, which young farmed fish eat.*

One reason people are overfishing in some areas is to catch wild fish to make fishmeal. Many fish farmers feed fishmeal to their growing fish. It takes about 3 tonnes (3.3 tons) of wild fish to produce fishmeal to feed just 1 tonne (1.1 ton) of farmed salmon.

Meat and fish

This graph shows how much beef and fish were farmed between 1950 and 2000. An average figure has been worked out by dividing the amount of farmed fish or beef produced during a year by the total world population.

What can we see from the graph?

• At present, more beef is produced than farmed fish.

• The number of farmed fish is increasing. Over 50 years it has risen from less than 1 kilogram (2.2 pounds) to 5 kilograms (11 pounds) per person.

• Beef production has only risen by about 1 kilogram (2.2 pounds) over the same period. However, overall it has been falling since about 1975.

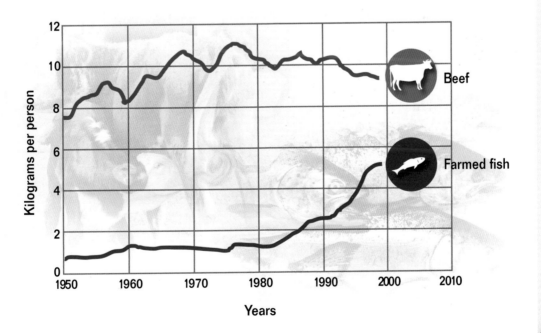

This graph compares the changes in beef farming and fish farming over the past 50 years.

{food and transport}

If you look at the information labels on food packets in your cupboard or fridge, you'll see that many of those foods come from a long way away.

Changing demand

The kinds of food that most people regularly eat have changed greatly over the last century. In the past most people ate local food that was in season. Today many people eat a wide range of foods from around the world at all times of the year.

We are able to eat all these different foods because transport has improved. In 1900 food could only be transported slowly by train or boat. Many foods, such as fruit, would have gone bad during long journeys. Today we have fast aeroplanes, ships, and lorries that can transport food quickly. Many have built-in fridges to keep food fresh.

FACT!

Amazingly, the average distance food travels before it reaches the shelf is 1,600 kilometres (nearly 1,000 miles).

*Supermarkets like this stock food **imported** from all over the world.*

Food transport problems

The machines people use to transport food are powered by engines that burn oil. When oil burns, it releases gases that make the air dirty and **polluted**. Air pollution causes many problems. It causes health problems in people. It mixes with rain to form **acid rain**, which damages plants and lakes. Air pollution damages the layers of air above the Earth, reducing the protection they give us from the Sun's harmful rays. It also traps the Sun's heat, causing **global warming**. Global warming is an increase in temperatures around the Earth.

Problems with packaging

People protect food from being squashed or knocked when it is transported by using packaging. Most packaging is made of plastic because it is light, can be moulded to the shape of the food, and is strong even if wet. When the food is used, the packaging is thrown away and becomes a waste problem. Plastic is very slow to rot so packaging waste collects on land and floats around the world's oceans.

*Here wheat grain is being loaded onto a ship. Many people argue that a lot of the food being transported long distances could be bought more locally to cut down on pollution and **fossil fuel** usage.*

{family farms}

About half the Earth's **population** mainly eats food that they grow themselves. This is called **subsistence farming**. Subsistence farmers live in the countryside in **less-developed countries,** such as many parts of Africa and Asia.

Farming methods

Subsistence farmers tend to the land using simple tools. For example, they use oxen instead of tractors to pull ploughs. **Fertile** land is usually shared between lots of people. This means that fields are small. Many subsistence farmers can only grow enough food if the whole family, from young children to grandparents, helps.

In good years, with enough rain and sun, subsistence farmers might harvest many **crops** or raise lots of **livestock**. They may be able to sell some of their produce. Often families go hungry. Too much rain can flood their fields, whereas not enough rain may make crops wither and die and leave livestock thirsty.

*In many countries, children fetch wild plants to feed livestock, collect animal dung to **fertilize** soil, or water crops before and after school. These children are picking cotton bolls from cotton plants at their family farm.*

Poverty

Subsistence farmers usually have too little money to go out and buy food, medicines, or new clothes, so in bad years they may go without altogether. They rarely have enough money to buy fertilizers to make the land more fertile and increase the amount of crops they can grow. Some children do so many farm chores that they do not have time to go to school. Then they do not learn to read and write and find it more difficult to learn new skills.

FACT!

In Chad and many other African countries 80 percent or more of the population relies on subsistence farming and livestock raising for food and life. That is eight out of every ten people.

Subsistence farming around the world

This world map shows the areas where there are subsistence farmers, people who rely on farming to make a living. The lighter colours are where fewer people rely on farming. The darkest colours are areas where most people (80 to 100 percent) live on family farms. The horizontal lines across areas show where people go hungry.

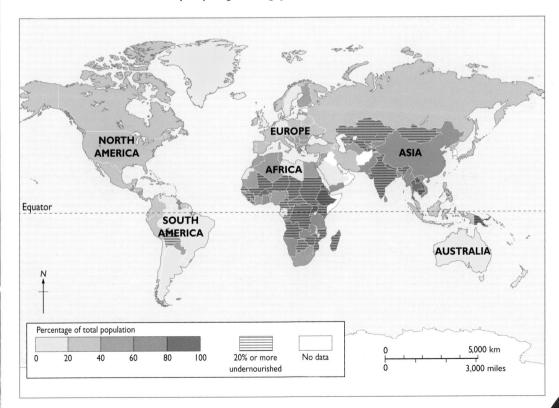

This map shows areas of the world where people rely on farming for a living.

{the changing face of farming}

In richer parts of the world, such as the USA or Europe, **subsistence farming** is rare. In these places, most food is grown using modern machines and techniques. These allow farmers to produce large amounts, more quickly. This is called **intensive farming** and farmers who use this method grow food to sell, not to eat themselves.

Modern crop growing

Intensive farming is farming on a big scale. **Crops** are grown in immense fields or giant greenhouses. Farmers use new varieties of plants that can produce more food, for example maize that makes more corn cobs or spinach plants that grow more leaves. As the plants grow, farmers spray on water, **fertilizers**, and other chemicals. These include **pesticides**, which kill insects that may eat the crop, and **herbicides**, which kill weeds growing among the crops. Sometimes farmers hire aeroplanes to spray crops because this is the quickest way to cover enormous fields.

In intensive farming, farmers use large, expensive machines. Here a giant combine harvester is being used to harvest crops of grain.

Livestock production

Livestock can also be farmed intensively. Farmers keep lots of animals together in one place. Farmers carefully control what the livestock eat to make sure they produce lots of the meat, eggs, and milk customers want. They feed the animals with grain but also special foods containing chemicals. These chemicals help the animals grow faster and with bigger muscles. These muscles become the meat we eat. The farmers inject animals with medicines to prevent illness. They make sure the animals have just enough heat, light, water, and bedding to be comfortable.

FACT!

In a large pig farm in the USA there might be half a million pigs in just one enormous shed.

More intensive

Since 1960, the percentage of people involved in farming around the world has dropped. One of the main reasons is the move towards intensive farming, because one machine can do the work of many people. In this graph we can see that in North America the proportion has dropped from 7 percent in 1960 to 3 percent in 2000. In Africa, it has dropped from 80 to 55 percent over the same period.

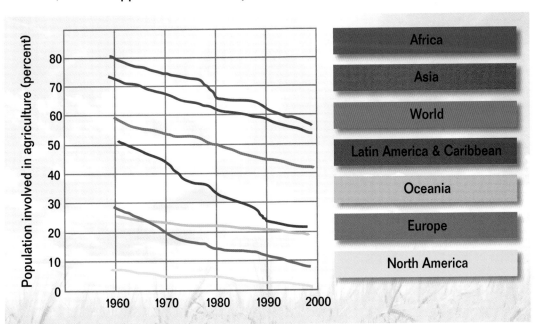

This graph shows the proportion of population involved in agriculture in different parts of the world.

{ problems with intensive farming }

Intensive farming has changed the world of farming. Many farmers now produce more food, more quickly and more cheaply than ever before. Modern chemicals have helped prevent failed **crops**, for example by making soil more **fertile** and by getting rid of insect pests. However, there are lots of problems with intensive farming.

Water problems

Some of the **fertilizers** that farmers spray on crops fall on the soil. When rain falls, it washes soil containing fertilizers into rivers, lakes, and seas. These fertilizers help tiny, plant-like **algae** in the water grow fast. When the algae die, **bacteria** that feed on them use up most of the **oxygen** in the water. This process is called eutrophication. Without oxygen in the water, animals, such as fish, cannot breathe and so they die.

FACT!

Nearly three-quarters of all the freshwater that people use in the world is taken by farmers to put on crops or give to **livestock**.

If agricultural chemicals get into rivers they can encourage a growth of algae that may kill river wildlife.

Pesticides and people

Traces of the chemicals that are sprayed on crops and fed to animals are often found on the food that we eat. In the USA, water in 6 percent of all wells contains unsafe amounts of fertilizer. In the UK, **pesticides** are found in nearly half of all milk and potatoes. Some scientists believe that these chemicals can be bad for our health.

Habitat problems

Farmers create massive fields by chopping down woodland and hedges between smaller fields. When they do this, they destroy important **habitats** where wildlife lives. For example, in the UK the loss of **hedgerows** has led to a decline in dormice, a hedgerow animal.

Farmers also drain wetlands, such as marshes, to farm the fertile soil beneath. Animals such as frogs and alligators need wet places to survive. When wetlands are destroyed, these animals may die because they cannot find new homes.

*About one-fifth of the planet's farmland is irrigated to grow crops. This **irrigation** system uses sprinklers to water fields.*

{organic farming}

Organic farms grow **crops** and raise animals without using chemicals made in factories, such as **fertilizers**. Organic farming is not a new idea. Up until around 50 years ago most farmers had no choice but to rely on nature to help their crops grow. Today many farmers are turning their backs on **intensive farming** techniques, and going organic again.

Why farm organically?

Organic farmers say you can see the difference their way of farming makes when you look around their fields and see butterflies, birds, and colourful flowers. **Pesticides** kill insects and other pests that eat crops, and when these bugs disappear, so do the animals that feed on them. **Herbicides** kill any plants that are not crops, including colourful wild flowers.

How does organic farming work?

If farmers want to sell their food as organic, they need to grow their crops and raise their **livestock** in careful ways. Instead of using chemicals, organic farmers can only add **compost** (rotted food and plant waste), manure from farm animals, and natural **minerals** to make soil **fertile**.

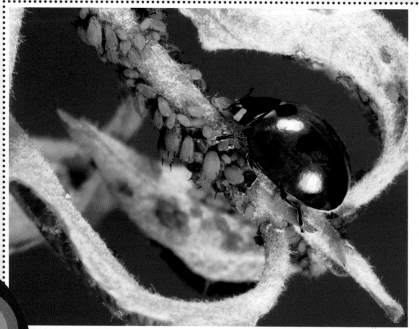

This ladybird is eating pests called aphids on an apple tree. By attracting insects that eat crop pests, organic farmers can avoid using pesticides.

Organic farmers grow plants that attract the kinds of insects that eat the pests that can damage crops. Animals kept on organic farms are fed on grain or other kinds of animal feed that are also organic. Farm animals are allowed to roam outside instead of being kept in pens for long periods of time. When they roam free they also eat large numbers of insects and slugs that might otherwise damage the farm's crops.

For and against

Many people believe organic food tastes better and that it is healthier to eat than food that may be **polluted** with chemicals. They like to buy organic food because they believe it is better for wildlife and for the natural world.

Other people are not so sure that organic farming is the way forward. They say that fields of intensively managed crops produce more food than organic fields so they can feed more people. Furthermore, at present, organic foods are more expensive to buy. Organic fruit and vegetables usually rot more quickly because they are not treated with chemicals to make them last longer.

Some animals, such as pigs and goats, are also excellent recyclers because they happily feed on leftover parts of crops.

{threats to farmland}

Farms today grow many more **crops** than they used to and produce vast amounts of food. However, at a time when the **population** is growing and people need more and more food, some farming methods and human activities are damaging farm soils. This reduces the amount of land people can use to grow food.

Spoiling soil

Topsoil, the layer of soil on the top of the land, is the **fertile** layer where plants grow. When topsoil becomes too dry, it can be blown or washed away. This kind of **erosion** is destroying many areas of farmland. Soil erosion can happen because of overgrazing, when too many animals eat the grass on an area of land.

FACT!

Healthy soil takes a long time to form. In some parts of the world soil is being worn out over 10,000 times faster than new soil can form to replace it.

The land in this part of China has turned to dust after being damaged by intensive farming methods.

Soil erosion also occurs because of heavy ploughing and digging, or the use of too many harsh chemical sprays. In some hot, dry areas big **irrigation** systems take so much water from the land that the soil dries up.

Spreading deserts

In some areas soil erosion has caused **desertification**. This is when soil becomes so dry, dusty, and low in **nutrients** that the land becomes desert. This is mainly a problem in countries that have hot, dry **climates**.

Soil degradation

At present about one-third of all the land across the world is used for farming. However, as soils around the world are degraded, or damaged, farmland is being lost. This map shows where on the planet the soil is degraded. Some areas have almost no plant life at all. This is mainly because this area is so very hot and dry. Soils that were once fertile and have been degraded are shown in red and orange.

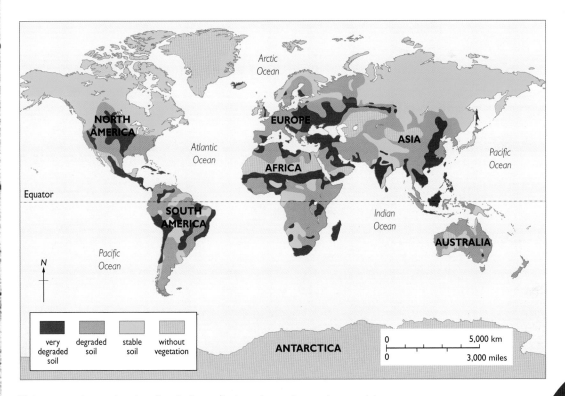

This map shows levels of soil degradation throughout the world.

{case study} lost farmland in Australia

Almost one-third of Australia's **fertile** farmland has disappeared over the last twenty years. **Intensive farming** methods are partly responsible for this disaster. Australia is one of the driest **continents** on Earth and most soils there are already dry. When **livestock** heavily **grazes** them or farm machines harshly plough them, the soils dry out even more. These dusty layers of soil then blow away. **Erosion** and the clearing of trees and other plants from land have also caused **desertification**.

Salt assault

The other problem Australian soil faces is salination. This is when people pump water out from deep under the ground and salts sometimes come up to the surface as well. Salt makes things dry out. That is why we cannot drink salty seawater and why plants die if you water them with seawater. When salty water ends up on the surface of the land, warm air dries it up. This leaves a layer of pure salt on the soil. The salt turns the soil as hard as rock and makes it useless for growing **crops**.

Hot and dry

Drought is also a problem for Australian farmers. Droughts are longer than usual periods of time without rain. During droughts, large areas of crops and **pasture** (grass) dry up and die. When crops fail, farmers struggle in two ways. They do not have crops to sell to make money and the price of grain and other animal food goes up. Many find they cannot afford to keep livestock and are forced to sell their cattle and sheep and give up farming altogether.

Drought and overgrazing kill off plants and leave the land bare.
Rain and wind may erode the top layer of soil, leaving dusty, useless earth.

{why are people hungry?}

We live in a world where 800 million people do not have enough to eat. One reason for this is that some countries do not have **fertile** soils or good conditions for growing **crops** and raising **livestock**. However, the problem is more complicated than this.

Poverty and hunger

In **less-developed countries** people grow their own food. They do not have enough money to buy machinery that could help them grow more. They cannot afford to buy food from other countries when their crops are killed by a natural disaster, such as **drought** or flooding, or they have to flee because of war.

The wrong kinds of food?

More than one-third of the world's grain is grown to feed livestock to provide some people with sausages, burgers, and other meat products. Many people argue that there would be enough food for all if we grew more **cereal** crops that people can eat.

Simple meals like this made up of only cereals or grains contain some nutrients that people need to stay healthy.

Too much, too little

While some people in the world do not have enough to eat, a large proportion of the **population** eat far too much!

This chart shows that the percentage of obese people in the USA is higher than the percentage of malnourished people in India. If you are obese it means you are so overweight that it is bad for your health. It usually means a person has been eating far too much of the wrong kinds of foods, such as sweets or cake that are high in sugars and fat and low in other **nutrients**. It usually also means they do not exercise enough. Most people who are obese have enough money to make choices about what they can eat, but they make the wrong choices.

When people are malnourished it means they don't have enough of the right foods to be healthy over a long period of time. In India there is enough food to feed everyone, but poor people don't have enough money to buy the variety of foods they need to be healthy.

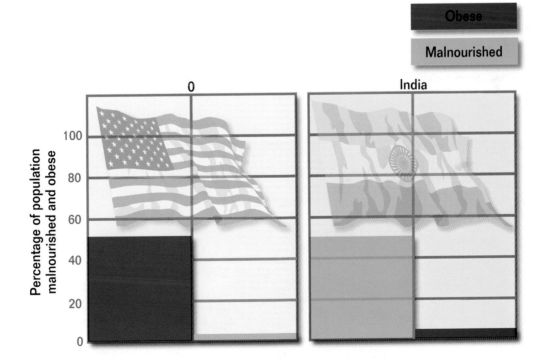

This chart compares the percentage of the population that is malnourished and obese in the USA and India.

{investigating ways to feed the world}

The number of people on Earth is steadily increasing. The world **population** is expected to rise from 6 billion to 8.3 billion by 2030. That would mean the world would need to produce almost half as much food again as we do now to feed everyone. All across the planet, food scientists and governments are investigating ways to make this happen.

GM foods

You have probably heard people mention **GM foods** on the news. GM stands for 'genetically modified'. Scientists create GM foods by changing, or modifying, certain **genes** in the seeds of **crops**. Genes are codes inside the **cells** of living things that make them the way they are. In people, genes decide whether we have blue, green, or brown eyes, or whether we are tall or short. In plants, genes control things like how tall they grow or how many seeds they produce.

*The purple cauliflower in this picture has been genetically modified to contain more **nutrients** than normal white cauliflowers.*

By altering a plant's genes, scientists can create new kinds of crops. They can make crops that do not get diseases or that have more nutrients than their natural equivalents. Or they can make more crops that can survive being sprayed with harmful chemicals, such as **pesticides**, or that stay fresher longer.

The GM debate

People in favour of GM foods believe they may help us feed the world. Those who are against them fear they could damage our health and the environment. They think production of GM foods should stop until scientists have been able to study the long-term effects of these foods.

One argument against GM foods is that GM seed-producing companies produce a very small number of different kinds of seeds. This means that many other varieties of corn, wheat, and rice, for example, are lost because people stop growing them. GM crops also require lots of chemicals to grow well. This makes the GM seed producers rich, but many people in **less-developed countries** cannot afford these chemicals.

This plant scientist is testing GM fruits to see if they are safe to eat.

{the future of agriculture}

Feeding the increasing number of people in the world is a huge challenge for the future. Science has some of the answers, but in some countries there may be other solutions.

The science of food

Many food scientists believe **GM foods** can solve future food shortages. GM foods that grow well with little water could be designed to grow in dry countries. GM fruit and vegetables that last longer and are easier to transport can be delivered further to feed more people.

Hydroponics

Hydroponics is a new way of growing **crops** without soil. Instead, plants are grown indoors in containers of water or gravel. Farmers make sure the plants get the right amounts of light, warmth, water, **oxygen**, and **nutrients** so they can guarantee lots of fruit and vegetables.

Sustainable farming

The future for farmers in **less-developed countries** may lie in sustainable farming methods. This kind of farming is designed to suit the weather and environment of a place. Farmers plant crops that grow well in local **climates**.

Many small farms around the world already use sustainable methods of farming. This organic farm uses sustainable farming methods to grow potatoes and mustard plants.

On sustainable farms, farmers grow a variety of crops to ensure local people get a balanced diet all year round. They use natural alternatives to chemicals, such as chilli and garlic, to keep pests away and grow perennials, which are plants that die back and regrow again the following year. This reduces the need for buying too many new seeds and **fertilizers** to get new plants growing.

Fair trade

People are hungry because they are poor. Many farmers are poor because foreign companies that buy the food they grow are not paying them a fair wage. Increasingly, people are becoming more concerned about where their food comes from. They choose to buy fair trade foods and products, made by farmers who get a fair wage for their work. That way they know when they eat something, the farmer who grew it and his family can eat well too.

More and more people are buying fresh food from local sources, such as farmers' markets. They like to know how and where it was grown. This also helps to reduce the environmental damage done by transporting food long distances.

43

{further resources}

Books

Earth's Changing Landscape: The Effects of Farming, Andrea Smith (Franklin Watts, 2003)

Farming, R. Thomson (Franklin Watts, 2004)

Try cooking your own food – it's fun! *Kids in the Kitchen*, Sara Lewis (Hamlyn, 2003), has hundreds of recipe ideas.

Websites

You can explore the Internet to find out more about food and agriculture. Websites can change, so if the links below no longer work use a reliable search engine.

UN Food and Agriculture Organization, an international agency helping to tackle the problem of hunger across the world: http://www.fao.org.

At Global Gang's website there is information and homework help on the topics of food and farming. Go to http://www.globalgang.org.uk/homeworkhelp/.

Find out more about food and fair trade at http://www.oxfam.co.uk.

Find out more about agriculture in the USA at http://www.fsa.usda.gov/ca/agforkids.htm. This site has game pages, fun facts, and useful things to print out and keep.

Tiki the penguin has a fun guide to food at http://tiki.oneworld.net

{glossary}

acid rain rainwater that has been polluted by chemicals in the air, making it acidic and damaging to wildlife

algae plant-like living thing which can be small as in the alga that floats on ponds or large as seaweed

bacteria tiny living things found everywhere, in air, water, soils, and food. Some bacteria are good for us; others can cause disease.

carbohydrate kinds of food that give you energy

cell smallest building block of all living things

cereals grain (seed) of different types of grasses, including wheat and rice

climate usual weather pattern in an area

compost rotted garden and food waste used on soil to make it fertile

continent any large mass of land on the Earth's surface

crop plant grown to sell as food or other products, such as rice and cotton

dairy product food made from milk such as cheese and yoghurt

delta triangular area of land where slow-moving river water meets the sea

desertification when soil becomes dry, dusty, and so low in nutrients that the land becomes desert

drought long period of time without rain or with too little rain

Equator imaginary line around the centre of the Earth

erosion wearing away of rock or soil, for example by wind or water

export transport and sell to other countries

exporter person who transports and sells food and other products to other countries

fertile describes soil that plants grow well in

fertilizers chemical powders, sprays, or liquids used to improve soil and help plants grow

food chain diagram that shows some of the living things that eat each other within a habitat (or food web) as links in a single chain (for example, grass>rabbit>fox)

fossil fuels fuels such as oil, coal, and gas. They formed from the remains of plants and animals that lived millions of years ago. They cannot be replaced.

fungi plant-like living things such as toadstools and mushrooms

gene information in all living things that controls the way they grow

global warming rise in temperatures across the world, caused by the greenhouse effect (blanket of gases in the air that are trapping heat)

GM food GM stands for 'genetically modified'. Scientists create GM foods by changing, or modifying, certain genes in the seeds of crops.

graze eat grass

habitat natural home of a group of plants and animals

hedgerow bushes that form a hedge

herbicides chemicals that kill weeds which grow among crops and steal their water and space

import buy food or goods from other countries

intensive farming farming on a big scale that uses large machines and many chemicals to produce more crops or livestock

irrigation supplying water through channels for crops

less-developed country country where many people are poor and do not have basic things like clean water or good schools

livestock farm animals such as cows, sheep, and goats

mineral substance such as iron, which is good for the health of living things in small amounts

monsoon rainy season in parts of Asia, Africa, and elsewhere

nutrients chemicals that plants and animals need to grow and survive

overfishing when too many of one kind of fish are taken from an area of sea

oxygen gas in the atmosphere that living things need to breathe in order to live

pasture grass for livestock (farm animals) to eat

pesticides chemicals used to kill insects and other crop pests

photosynthesis process by which plants make food in their leaves, using water, carbon dioxide from the air, and energy from sunlight

plantation large area of land covered with a single crop that can be harvested again and again

pollution something that poisons or damages air, water, or land

population number of people

protein nutrient in food that helps us grow and helps us heal when we are hurt

respiration process by which living things release energy from their food

subsistence farming describes farmers who grow only enough food for themselves and their families

temperate climate with warm, dry summers and cool, wet winters

topsoil upper, fertile layer of soil

tropical found in the tropics – countries around the Equator that have some of the hottest climates in the world

{index}

Titles in the *Geography Focus* series include:

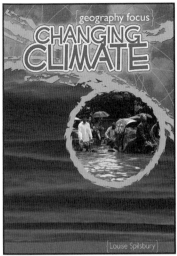

Hardback   1 74070 275 1
978 1 74070 275 1

Hardback   1 74070 278 6
978 1 74070 278 2

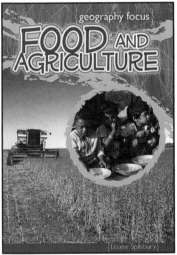

Hardback   1 74070 279 4
978 1 74070 279 9

Hardback   1 74070 277 8
978 1 74070 277 5

Hardback   1 74070 276 X
978 1 74070 276 8

Hardback   1 74070 274 3
978 1 74070 274 4

Find out about the other titles in this series on our website www.raintreepublishers.co.uk